Clues From PooS

Clues
From
Poos

Isabel Thomas

Contents

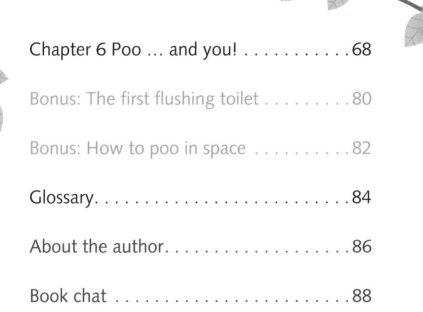

Chapter 1
What is poo?

Dung. Droppings. **Manure**. Whatever people call it, you probably know that they're talking about poo. Although it can be embarrassing to talk about, poo is something that all animals do every day. This includes humans, too – from world leaders, movie stars and astronauts, to the person sitting next to you.

Poo is an important part of every animal's life. For some animals, poo is the source of life! Studying poo helps scientists to understand and solve some of the world's most important problems.

Let's get to the bottom of the secret science of poo!

Whose poo?

Poo is the undigested waste food that has left an animal's body. It's full of clues that can tell us what an animal has eaten. Look carefully at the clues in these poos. Can you guess what animal they belong to?

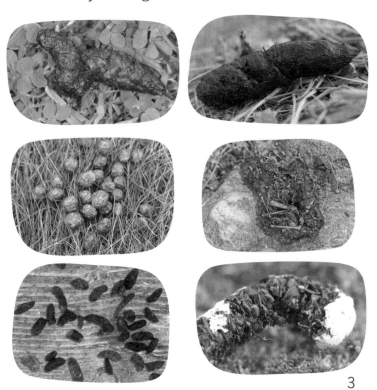

Hedgehogs have some of the prettiest poos. Their droppings often sparkle with pieces of beetle shell.

Fox poos are often full of fur, bones and berries. They have a pointed, twisty end.

Rabbit droppings are packed with grass, which makes them look yellow or green.

If you spot fish bones
and scales, you're probably
looking at an otter dropping.

Bat droppings
are full of
chewed-up insects.

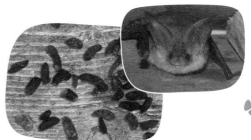

Green woodpecker
poos are often full
of dead ants.

These owl pellets are
not poos. Owls **regurgitate**
bones, fur or feathers through
their mouths.

Not
a poo!

5

How does food become poo?

The story of a poo begins the moment an animal swallows some food. Food contains energy and **nutrients** that the animal needs to live and grow. To get hold of these things, the animal's body must break the food down into tiny pieces. This is called digestion.

An animal's digestive system is a long tube that takes food on a journey from top to bottom. As food travels along this tube, it is crushed, dissolved and broken down. The useful bits are soaked up into the animal's blood. Gradually, most of the water is soaked up too. Anything that can't be digested exits through the animal's bottom.

stomach

bottom

intestines

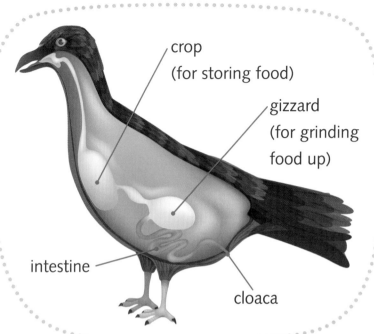

crop
(for storing food)

gizzard
(for grinding food up)

intestine

cloaca

Birds don't waste a drop of water, so their wee looks like white paste. The white part of a bird "poo" is really bird wee. Both come out through the same opening, called a cloaca.

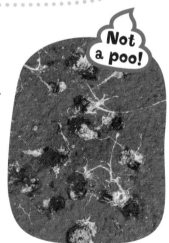

Not a poo!

Double digestion

For some animals, digestion doesn't end when they poo.

At night, rabbits and hares do soft, dark droppings which they eat immediately.

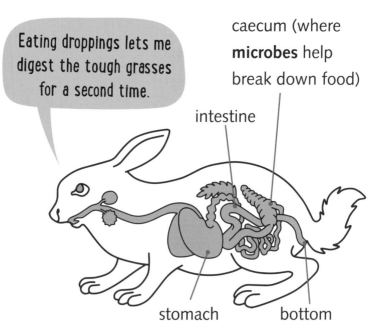

Eating droppings lets me digest the tough grasses for a second time.

caecum (where **microbes** help break down food)

intestine

stomach

bottom

These soft droppings still contain lots of water and undigested grass. After digesting this for a second time, the rabbit does hard, dry droppings.

soft poo   hard poo

Although some animals do poos that are safe for them to eat, it's never a good idea for a human to go near poo of any kind. Luckily, scientists study it for us, so that we don't have to!

An animal's intestines make slimy mucus to help food move smoothly along its digestive system and out of its body. The larger the animal, the thicker the mucus. This is why fresh animal poos often look a bit slimy.

Yuck!

What's in a poo?

Poo is the waste that is left behind after food has been digested. The parts of plants that can't be digested are known as fibre. Although animals can't digest fibre, it's an important thing for them to eat. Fibre helps food move through an animal's digestive system. It keeps the digestive system working well.

Poo contains lots of fibre. It also contains other types of undigested food, water and chemicals from the animal's digestive system.

The exact ingredients of a poo depend on what the animal eats. Herbivores (animals that eat plants) produce poos packed with plant fibre. Animals that eat meat produce poos with more protein (and a worse smell!).

Poo is a way for animals to get rid of anything their body doesn't need or want. Young lobsters poo out the deadly stingers from the jellyfish that they eat!

In autumn, European brown bears guzzle berries as they get ready to **hibernate**. Their poos can look and smell like a berry smoothie!

Yuck!

11

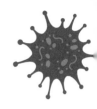

Poo is partly alive

An animal's digestive system is warm, dark and full of food. This makes it a perfect habitat for living things. All animals – including humans – have billions of microbes living inside their digestive system. Microbes are so small that we can't see them without a microscope. However, there are so many of them that they can have a big impact on our bodies.

Most of the microbes that live inside an animal's intestines are "friendly" – they don't do any harm to their host. They even help their host to digest food. However, sometimes unfriendly microbes get into our digestive systems. Unfriendly microbes are known as "germs" and they can make us ill.

Every time an animal poos, some of the microbes from its intestines are pooed out too. This includes friendly microbes, but it might include unfriendly germs too.

Washing our hands gets rid of any tiny germs, so they don't get onto our food and into our bodies.

We can keep ourselves safe by washing our hands after:

- touching soil (which might contain animal poo)
- cleaning up a pet's poo
- going to the toilet ourselves, even if we don't poo.

13

Plastic found in animal poo

Tiny pieces of plastic have been found in the poo of wild animals for the first time.

Scientists at the University of Georgia in the US have found plastic in the poo of wild fur seals. The seals live on a remote island near South

America, far from places where plastic is made or used. The pieces of plastic found in the seals' poo are so small that they can only be seen under a microscope. These tiny microfibres have come from some of our clothes that have been made with plastic. When we wash our clothes, these microfibres get into the water. Eventually, they end up in rivers and seas.

Tiny sea creatures mistake plastic microfibres for food. Later on, they are eaten by crabs and fish, which are then eaten by seals.

Scientists don't yet know if the plastic harms fur seals. But testing animal poo will be a useful way to measure how much plastic pollution is in the oceans.

Chapter 2
Poo on the menu

Every poo contains some undigested food. Rabbits aren't the only animals whose droppings are safe for them to eat in order to digest their food for a second time.

Rodents

Mice, rats, hamsters, guinea pigs and naked mole rats are all rodents, and they all eat their own droppings. This gives them a second chance to get hold of nutrients and energy. It also puts friendly microbes back into their bodies.

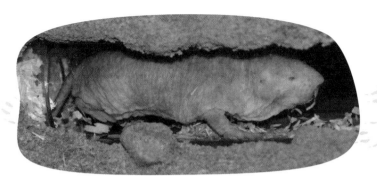

Naked mole rats eat the tough parts of plants that grow underground. They rely on friendly microbes to help digest their food. Millions of these microbes leave their body each time they poo. Eating their own poos helps naked mole rats to get these microbes back.

Guinea pigs are rodents too. Like rabbits, they do special, soft poos that are safe for them to eat. Guinea pigs can gobble up to 50 of these pellets in an hour, and it helps to keep them healthy!

Snack time

Next time you complain about your dinner, spare a thought for the young animals whose parents give them poo to eat! They include cassowaries, giant birds that live in Australia. Cassowary chicks often peck pieces of fruit out of their parents' poo! This helps the chicks to get the nutrients they need. It also helps them to get hold of the microbes they need to digest fresh fruits themselves.

Koala and panda mothers feed their poo to their babies. Baby elephants and hippos also eat poo from their parents, and even from other members of their herd! This is a quick way for them to get the microbes that they need to help them digest tough leaves.

Most of the animals that can safely eat their own poo are herbivores (plant-eaters). Most carnivores (meat-eaters) don't do this, because their poos are more likely to contain dangerous germs.

Dung for dinner

There is one animal that eats so much dung, it's named after it! Dung beetles live on every continent in the world, except Antarctica. There are thousands of different kinds, but they all share a love of herbivore poo. The fresher the better. From a dung beetle's point of view, an elephant is a giant food van.

Within minutes of an elephant doing a poo, dung beetles fly in and begin to feast. They don't chew up the solid parts of the poo. They suck out the juices, which are rich in nutrients.

In some parts of the world, butterflies
can also be spotted sipping juices from piles
of dung. This is known as "mud-puddling".
It helps the butterflies to get nutrients and salts
that aren't found in their normal foods.

Marine Snow

Seas and oceans are full of animals, which means they are also full of poo. The white coloured droppings from billions of fish and other creatures sink slowly towards the seabed, like a never-ending snowfall.

Deep-sea creatures, such as vampire squid, gobble up this "marine snow" as it drifts past. Animals that are fixed in place, such as sponges, filter it out of the water.

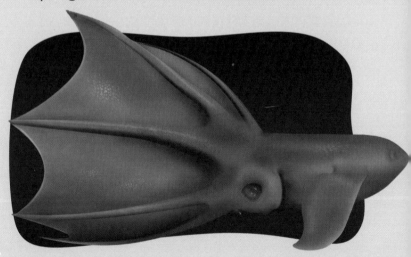

Vampire squid don't live up to their name. They eat poo, not blood. Their "ears" are actually tools to help them catch marine snow.

Eventually, marine snow settles on the ocean floor. Creatures that crawl across the seabed, such as sea cucumbers, hoover it up. In the deep ocean, where there is no light, marine snow is one of the main foods that animals can find.

Cave diving

Poo is also an important food for animals that
live in dark caves. Plants can't grow in the dark,
so bats and birds collect food from outside.
When they return to the cave for shelter, huge
piles of droppings form below their roosts.
Insects such as beetles and cockroaches, and
other small animals such as millipedes, feast
on these droppings. Larger cave animals
such as snakes and spiders, then eat these
smaller animals.

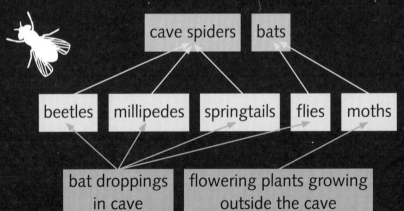

cave spiders   bats

beetles   millipedes   springtails   flies   moths

bat droppings
in cave

flowering plants growing
outside the cave

A feast for fungi

Fungi are living things that are not plants or animals. They can't make their own food, like plants do. They can't move around nibbling food, like animals do. Instead, fungi soak their food up from whatever they are growing on.

Lots of fungi like to grow and feed on poo!

One of these is hairy poop mould. It quickly appears on animal droppings, making them look furry or fuzzy. Hairy poop mould isn't fussy; it will grow on almost any kind of poo. It can also be found on other things that are decaying, such as fallen leaves.

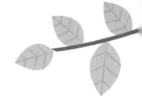

From poo to plate

"How disgusting," you might be thinking. "I'd never eat poo." In fact, humans do eat foods that are made with the help of poo! All these foods are made carefully so they are safe to eat.

Certain types of tea and coffee are made using coffee beans or tea leaves that have passed all the way through the digestive system of an animal, such as a panda or a caterpillar. The partly digested beans or leaves are collected from the animals' poo.

Most mushrooms that humans eat are farmed on compost made from waste – including manure, which is herbivore poo that has been turned into compost!

Even desserts can be made with the help of poo! Castoreum is a food ingredient that smells just like vanilla. Real vanilla comes from the seed pods of orchid plants. Castoreum comes from the bottoms of beavers.

How long does it take to do a poo?

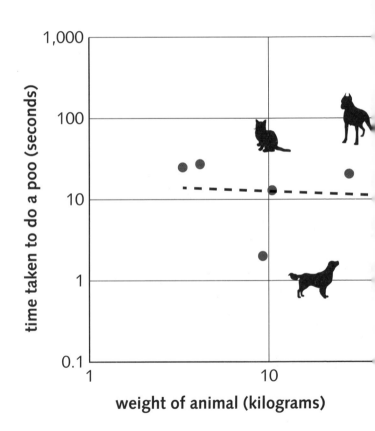

Mammal poos come in all shapes and sizes. However, scientists have discovered that all mammals take around 12 seconds to do a poo, no matter how big or small they are!

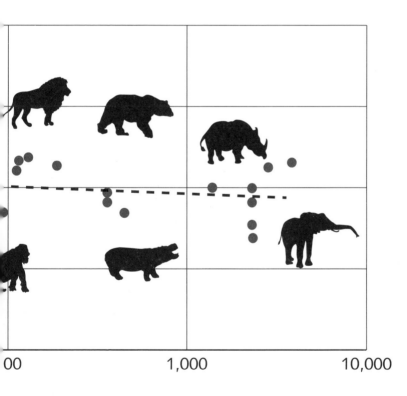

00   1,000   10,000

Chapter 3
101 things to do with a poo

In nature, nothing goes to waste – not even waste! In the animal kingdom, poo is not just used as food. It's used for communication and camouflage, to build homes and as a weapon. One animal is even known to use crocodile poo as make-up and whale poo as perfume!

Let's meet the creatures that know how to get more from manure.

Stinky childcare

Piles of manure covered in dung beetles are a common sight around the world. But the beetles aren't just there to suck out the delicious juices. Some can be spotted making balls of manure, which they roll away and bury underground. The beetles lay their eggs inside these balls. When the larvae (baby beetles) hatch out, they have the dung all to themselves – an edible bedroom!

Dung beetles shape and roll balls of dung weighing up to 50 times their own weight! They push the balls along with their back legs, climbing on top to cool down if the ground gets too hot.

In some parts of the world, eight in every ten piles of manure are buried by dung beetles. Without them, the ground would be covered in dried-out dung.

Lots of flies also like to breed on dung. Look out for male yellow dung flies hanging out on fresh cowpats or sheep droppings.

They aren't interested in eating the poo – they are predators that eat other insects. As well as looking for a meal of smaller insects, these male yellow dung flies also hang out on poo waiting for a female fly to come along to mate with.

Females like to lay their eggs in dung, so the larvae (baby flies) will have something to eat when they hatch out. As well as food, the dung helps to protect the larvae, because most other animals avoid poo!

Houseflies and bluebottles also like to lay their eggs on dung. If they can't find fresh poo, the flies will settle for food that is left lying around.

Yuck!

Tricks and traps

Caterpillars have huge appetites, and the more they eat, the more they poo. The problem is that a trail of droppings would show predators, like wasps, exactly where to find the caterpillar. To solve this problem, skipper caterpillars catapult their poo up to 40 body lengths away, leading wasps to the wrong place.

Burrowing owls take the opposite approach. They line their burrows with the poo of other animals. This helps them to lure insects, such as dung beetles, inside – which they then gobble up.

Wolves love rolling in animal poo – especially the poo of larger predators, such as big cats and bears. Scientists have lots of ideas to explain this disgusting habit. It may be to disguise themselves from prey, to keep insects away, or as super-stinky camouflage to help them hide from predators.

The caterpillars of giant swallowtail butterflies look just like bird droppings. This puts birds off taking a bite.

Orchard spiders live on fruit trees, where they can feast on moths at night. By day, they sit hunched on a leaf, looking just like a bird dropping.

Of course, you've already met animals –
such as flies – that DO love to eat poo. To deter
these, this moth has a wing pattern that looks
like a bird dropping being eaten by two flies
who got there first!

Even frogs are in on this trick. The bird
poo frog can hang out on a leaf without fear,
because it looks so much like a revolting poo.

Communication

Wombats are the only animals on the planet whose poos have corners. These cube-shaped droppings don't roll away, so wombats can place them in careful piles, which they use to communicate with other wombats.

White rhinos use poo to help them stay in touch. By sniffing piles of poo, rhinos can tell which other rhinos have visited, how healthy they are, and if they want to breed.

Naked mole rats poo in special "rooms" in their underground burrows, and roll around in the poo that collects there. The smell helps them to identify each other in the dark.

Making buildings

Termites use a mixture of their poo and spit to build walls inside their giant nests. The cement-like mixture helps to make their mounds ten times stronger than soil alone.

Cooling their feet

Vultures and storks poo on their own legs when it's hot. The water in the poo evaporates like sweat, cooling them down.

Anti-aging

Scientists in Germany discovered
that fish live longer by eating
the poo of younger fish.
This disgusting dinner
contains friendly microbes
from the intestines of
the younger fish. The microbes may help
to protect the older fish from diseases.

Egyptian vultures also use poo as
a beauty treatment. Their main food is rotting
meat, but by snacking on yellow cow poo,
they top up on the vitamins needed
to keep their beaks and faces
bright yellow. These are
the same vitamins
found in carrots!

Last but not least, which animal uses crocodile droppings as face cream and whale poo as perfume? It turns out to be ... humans! Some Ancient Romans used a face powder made from crocodile poo. A waxy substance called ambergris – found in the poo of sperm whales – has been used to make expensive perfumes for more than a thousand years.

It's the secret to my good looks.

Chapter 4
Our planet depends on poo

You've met creatures that use poo in different ways, but did you know that almost EVERY creature depends on poo? Most of Earth's habitats are made of the stuff!

Next time you spot an earthworm in the garden, stop and watch for a while.

You're looking at one of the most important animals in the world. There are almost 3,000 different kinds of earthworms, but they all burrow through the ground eating decaying matter and pooing out waste. This poo is an important part of soil.

Earthworms create soil AND make sure it stays in good condition. Without them, farming – and life as we know it – would be impossible. The largest earthworm ever found was almost seven metres long. Imagine the size of its poos!

Nature's caretakers

Lots of other animals, known as detritivores, also feed on dead plants. They include millipedes, woodlice and snails. They speed up decay by quickly converting dead plants into poo.

Whale-sized poos

Poo is just as important in ocean ecosystems. Whales catch and eat huge amounts of food in the deep seas, then rise to the surface where they do gigantic poos. These poos contain important **minerals** which small creatures near the sea's surface need to be healthy. Whales are the gardeners of the ocean, fertilising the water so new life can grow.

A blue whale can release 200 litres of poo in one go! That's enough to fill a bathtub.

Poo turns up on the beach too. Which of these pictures looks like poo to you?

Yuck!

The answer is: both of them!

The squiggles of sand that appear on beaches at low tide are piles of lugworm poo. These bristly worms hide in the sand, in U-shaped burrows. They swallow sand, digest tiny specks of food mixed with it, and poo out the rest.

Coral reefs are covered in **algae**, which make a good meal for parrotfish. These colourful fish chip off chunks of coral with their tough teeth, grind it up in their guts, digest the algae and poo out white coral sand. A single parrotfish can produce almost a tonne of sand in a year!

Yuck!

Around three-quarters of white sand
tropical beaches are made up of fish poo.

Seed spreaders

Have you ever wondered why plants go to the trouble of making delicious fruits? They are trying to get their seeds eaten by animals – and pooed out somewhere else!

Most plants that make fruits rely on animals to spread their seeds. The further a seed starts growing from its parent plant, the better. It means the new plants don't have to compete for light, water and space. Beginning life in a pile of poo is not a problem for seeds. In fact, dung is a great **fertiliser**!

Ripe fruits are often brightly coloured to help animals find them among green leaves. They are also juicy and soft, so animals can swallow them without chewing. The soft pulp gets digested, but the seeds are protected by a tough coat, so they survive.

One South African grass plant uses a different poo-related trick to get its seeds spread. It produces seeds that look and smell just like antelope droppings. Dung beetles rush to roll away and bury the seeds, accidentally acting as gardeners for the grass.

Not a poo!

A manure mystery

Sloths live very slow lives, hanging upside down from tree branches. They eat, sleep and even give birth in the trees. In fact, sloths only leave their tree for one reason: to poo!

This journey is dangerous. By coming down to the ground to poo, sloths are more likely to be spotted by predators. It also uses up precious energy. Why take the risk?

Scientists have several hypotheses:

- Pooing on the ground could help sloths to fertilise the trees they live in.
- It could be a way to keep in touch with other sloths.
- It could help more algae to grow on the sloth's fur.

When sloths visit the ground to poo, moths that live in their fur get a chance to lay their eggs in the fresh dung. More eggs means more moths, and more moths leads to more algae growing on a sloth's fur. Algae is an important source of food for the sloths, and a helpful camouflage in the tree tops.

Too much poo

Poo is an important part of almost every ecosystem on Earth. However, if too much poo is put in one place, it can cause problems.

When humans keep large numbers of animals on farms, the animals produce a huge amount of waste. If that poo gets washed into rivers, lakes or seas, it acts as a fertiliser for tiny algae. So many algae grow that they can change the colour of the water. This is called an algal bloom.

The algae block light from getting to plants that grow underwater. The algae also use up most of the oxygen in the water, and this harms animals that live in the water. People that rely on rivers or lakes can also be harmed by **toxic** algae. People who rely on fishing might lose their source of food.

The lake in this picture has turned green because so many algae are growing in it. The algae feed on animal waste that has been washed into the water.

Poo is an important part of a healthy planet. However, when people disturb the natural balance, it can cause problems.

Poo detective

Look at these poos. What clues are there about the animals that left them?

Chapter 5
Clues from poos

Poo is helping scientists solve all kinds of mysteries. It can reveal secret penguin hideaways and help keep monkeys healthy. Poo is even being used to answer questions about the past.

Staring at poo from space

It's not easy to count penguins. Most live in Antarctica, in the coldest place on the planet. So scientists are turning to poo to help them track and count penguins!

Penguins poo all day long, staining the Antarctic snow and ice. The poo stains made by huge penguin colonies are so big they are visible from space.

By scanning pictures taken by **satellites** in space, scientists can find new colonies and estimate how many penguins live in them.

This method has revealed that there are millions more penguins in Antarctica than scientists once thought. We can also compare poo pictures from previous years, to see how climate change is affecting penguin populations.

Clues from birds

Bird droppings reveal where birds like to roost. They are helping scientists to find out what birds do in the daytime too.

One team of scientists collected 200 bird droppings from the same group of songbirds, before and after they made a long journey for the summer.

They found that when the birds changed location, the microbes in their droppings changed too. It showed how the different food they ate in each area affected their health.

When large groups of seabirds gather in the Arctic in summer, they poo so much that it paints rocks white. Scientists have found out that this poo helps to cool the Arctic. As the poo rots, it releases a chemical called ammonia, which helps clouds to form. The clouds keep off the sunlight and help to keep the ground cooler.

Zoo poo clue

When an animal is ill, vets look closely at
the animal's poos to help find out what
is wrong. Poo even helped to solve the mystery
of why some monkeys in a zoo were getting
ill, while other monkeys living in the same
enclosure were fine.

At first everyone was puzzled. Then, a scientist
decided to look at the monkey poo under
a microscope. They saw that some of
the monkeys had been nibbling a dangerous
plant that grew just outside their enclosure.

The sharp leaves were
damaging their
digestive systems.
The clue in the poo
saved these
monkeys' lives.

Human poo clues

It's hard to imagine one of your own poos taking pride of place in a museum. But ancient human poos are helping archaeologists find out about human history too.

Scientists found traces of 7,300-year-old human poo in rock collected from an ancient lake. Substances found in the prehistoric poo tell us what humans were doing and eating back then. The amount of poo even tells us how big their communities were.

Poo from today's humans is full of important clues too. When someone is ill, viruses are often found in their poo. By taking samples of sewage from a city, and measuring the number of viruses, scientists can work out how quickly diseases are spreading.

61

Poo from the past

Dinosaurs have been extinct for millions of years. How do scientists know so much about them? They look for clues – including fossilised dinosaur poos!

Fossil poos are known as coprolites. The shape and size of a coprolite tells us which ancient animal it came from. Coprolites tell us what these animals ate too. They might contain fossils of smaller animals and plants, which helps scientists work out if a dinosaur ate meat, or plants, or both. Teeth marks on the fossils inside a coprolite can even tell us how the dinosaur ate its prey!

One of the largest coprolites ever found was once a Tyrannosaurus rex dropping the size of a human leg! It is full of crunched-up bones.

Ancient bird poo is a good place to look for clues too. A thousand years ago, giant birds called moa used to live in New Zealand. Today the moa is extinct, but it's still possible to find their fossilised coprolites. Scientists have found tree seeds in these coprolites, telling us that moa were important for spreading tree seeds and helping forests to grow.

Poo's part in history

Fossils have revealed that dung beetles may have been around to eat dinosaur dung. We won't know for sure until we find a fossil of a dung beetle and a dinosaur poo together.

Historians have been working on a different dung mystery. They wanted to know why dung beetles were so important to ancient Egyptians. Paintings and models of the beetles – known as scarabs – have been found in many ancient Egyptian **tombs**. They were even placed inside a mummy, close to its heart.

Why did the ancient Egyptians spend so much time celebrating insects that spend their lives in poo? One idea is that the way the beetles roll balls of dung may have reminded the ancient Egyptians of the daily cycle of the sun as it rolls across the sky. This would make the sun a massive ball of dung!

Dung beetles do also use the sun to help them navigate. They push dung towards the sun to make sure they travel in a straight line. They want to move the dung away from the dung pile, so other beetles don't steal it! When they climb on a ball of dung and "dance", they are looking for a clear path.

Mary Anning's coprolites

Fossil hunter Mary Anning was one of the first people to work out that coprolites were the fossilised dung of extinct animals. These are drawings of some of the coprolites she found.

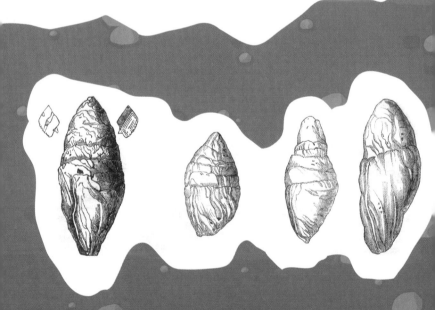

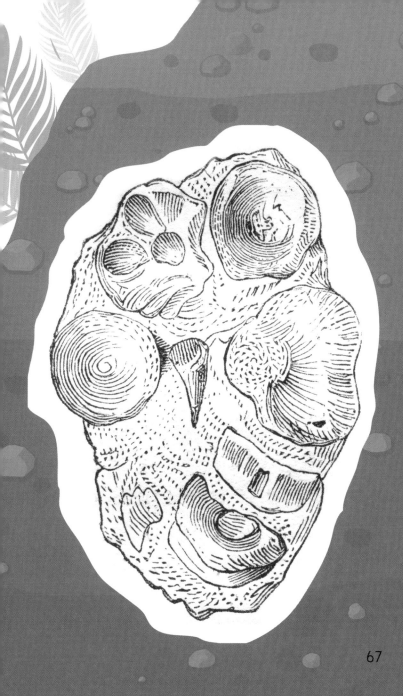

Chapter 6
Poo ... and you!

Poo helps plants, animals and every other creature on our planet. Humans are good at finding clever uses for poo too.

Poo power

The undigested food in poo contains energy. For thousands of years, people have burnt dried animal dung as fuel to heat their homes and to cook food. Poo will be an important fuel of the future, too.

Today, both human and animal poo can be collected and used to make methane gas.

This "biogas" is just as useful as the natural gas piped to homes, schools and offices. It can be burnt to heat water, cook food or generate electricity.

Natural gas is a fossil fuel, which can't be replaced once it has been used. Using methane from human and animal poo is much kinder to the planet than using fuel that comes from non-renewable sources, like coal and oil. The methane from poo can also be used to make hydrogen gas, which is increasingly used for heating, lighting and many other things.

Buses were some of the first vehicles to run on methane made from waste and poo. The first biogas bus could travel up to 300 kilometres on one tank of fuel (made from a year's worth of poo from a family of five people). Today, hundreds of UK buses, trucks and bin lorries run on methane.

From poo to barbeque?

Scientists are working on new ideas to turn poo into power. One team has invented a solar-powered toilet that turns poo into small bricks that can be burnt like the charcoal we use on barbeques. In the future, inventions like this could use poo to heat and power millions of homes around the world.

One day, poo could even provide power in space. Scientists have suggested that bases on the Moon or Mars could convert poo into rocket fuel for trips back to Earth.

So far, humans haven't been good at clearing up after themselves in space. Astronauts on the first Moon missions left behind 96 bags full of poo and wee.

Yuck!

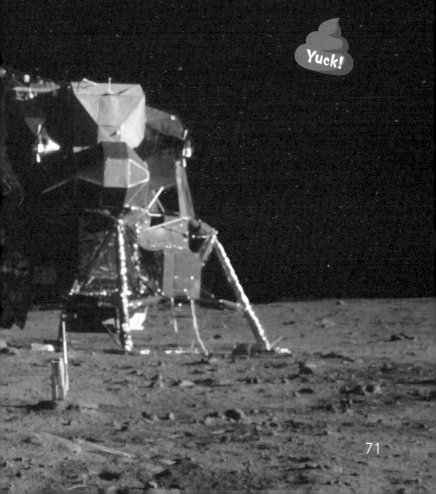

Poo bricks

In history lessons, we learn that a mixture of mud and manure was once used to build homes. But did you know that poo is also being used to make modern building bricks?

In one Australian experiment, scientists used sewage sludge to replace a quarter of the clay used to make bricks. The bricks were just as strong as normal bricks but took less energy to make.

More than 1.5 trillion clay bricks are made around the world every year. Replacing some of the clay with poo could help to save a huge amount of energy.

One water company in the UK plans to use sewage sludge to make large building blocks. The poo from four million people will help to make 2.3 million of these blocks every year. Imagine your poo becoming part of a new school or a skyscraper!

Farmers' friends

Adding poo to soil helps plants to grow. Farmers have been doing this for thousands of years.

Bird droppings, known as guano, make great fertiliser. It contains lots of phosphorus, which is good for growing plants. The world's 800 million seabirds poo out about 99,000 tonnes of phosphorus every year.

Back in the 1800s, guano was big business. It was collected from islands where seabirds roosted and shipped around the world to spread on fields. It was even nicknamed "white gold". Bat guano has also been mined from caves for hundreds of years.

Today, farmers are more likely to use **artificial** fertilisers, but guano mining still happens in some parts of the world. It is carefully controlled because it could harm the habitats of bats and birds.

Human poo can also be used as fertiliser if it's made safe first. In the US, for example, more than half of the solid sludge left over from sewage treatment plants is treated to kill any germs, then spread on fields.

Another way to turn human waste into fertiliser is to let worms feed on the poo, converting it to compost in just a few months. This could help to solve another problem too.

More than 892 million people around the world don't have access to safe toilets with running water. Special composting toilets could pay for themselves, by producing fertiliser for farming. Composting toilets don't use running water to flush poo away. Instead, they collect the poo, which is eaten by worms. The worms turn the poo into safe compost which can be spread on fields to fertilise crops.

Poo on prescription

Remember all those friendly microbes that live inside our intestines? We don't normally notice they're there, but we couldn't digest food without them. They help to keep us healthy in other ways too.

Doctors have learnt that our friendly microbes are so important, we can become ill if we don't have enough, or don't have the right types. They are beginning to treat some illnesses by moving a small amount of poo from a healthy person into the intestines of the patient. This gives the sick person a brand-new army of friendly microbes.

Mining for minerals

Scientists still have plenty of poo problems
to solve. One of these is hidden in the sludge
that collects in sewers. It contains tiny traces
of precious metals, such as copper and gold.
These specks are too small to see, but
the metals in the sewage from a million people
could be worth more than ten million pounds.
Someone still needs to work out how to get
hold of them. Become a scientist or engineer,
and that someone could be you!

The first flushing toilet

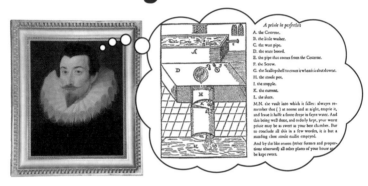

The first flushing toilet was invented by John Harington more than 400 years ago. Before then, people sat on seats above a pan or bucket, which had to be emptied by hand. Harington's toilet emptied itself! Water was pumped up into a tank called a cistern, behind the seat. When the handle was turned, the water flowed down into the pan and washed its contents into a cesspit underneath.

A privie in perfection

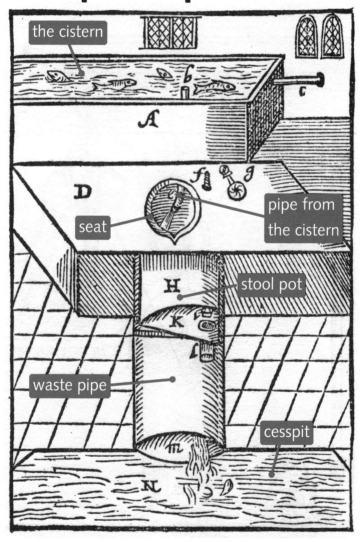

the cistern

seat

pipe from the cistern

stool pot

waste pipe

cesspit

How to poo in space

This is NASA's new Universal Waste Management System – also known as a space toilet!

If you ever find yourself on the International Space Station, here's what to do.

1. Lift the lid to start air flowing, helping to stop the smell from spreading through the space station.

2. Then position yourself over the small seat (it isn't easy to do in **microgravity**!). Use the foot straps and handholds to keep yourself in place.

3. After you wee into the funnel or poo into the container, make sure to put the used toilet paper into sealed bags!

Astronaut wee is cleaned and recycled into drinking water. Astronaut poo is stored until it can be loaded onto a special cargo ship that falls back to Earth and burns up on re-entry. Next time you see a "shooting star", remember that it could be burning astronaut poo!

Glossary

algae tiny plant-like creatures that can make their own food using the energy in sunlight

artificial made by humans, instead of being found in nature

fertiliser a substance added to soil to help plants grow better or faster

hibernate when an animal spends cooler months in a special kind of sleep, so they use less energy than usual

intestines the part of an animal's digestive system that carries food from the stomach to the anus; as it travels along the intestines, useful things in food pass into the animal's blood

manure animal dung that is used as a fertiliser

microbes tiny living things that can only be seen with a microscope

microgravity the very weak gravity felt by astronauts orbiting Earth

minerals substances formed in the earth that are not animals or plants

nutrients things that a living thing needs to take in, in order to live and grow

prescription a written instruction from a doctor that says a patient can be given a certain type of medicine or treatment

regurgitate when an animal brings food they have swallowed back up into their mouth

satellites spacecraft that are sent into orbit around a planet to send back information

tombs special buildings or spaces for burying people who have died

toxic poisonous

About the author

A bit about me …

I've written more than 250 books, and most of them are about science and nature! When I'm not writing, I like bouldering (indoor climbing) and going on adventures with my three children.

Isabel Thomas

How did you get into writing?

At university, I started writing for a student newspaper. It was the first time I thought about writing as a job. The experience also helped me to get my first job as a writer.

What is it like for you to write?

It feels a bit like doing a jigsaw puzzle when you don't know what the final picture will look like. I concentrate so much that I forget about everything else. I'm always moving words and sentences around, until everything fits together perfectly.

What is a book you remember loving reading when you were young?

I had a huge nature encyclopedia with a missing jacket, so I'm not sure what it actually looked like. It just had the plain green cover. I realised that if I used information from the book in my homework, writing it in my own words, I would get really good marks! It was my first introduction to research.

Why did you decide to write this book?

When I visit schools, children always ask me curious questions about poo. Scientists are also asking questions about poo! I decided to combine all this amazing research in one book.

What do you hope readers will get out of the book?

I hope that readers will get a better understanding of something we all do – poo! I also hope to spread the word that scientists investigate ANYTHING that makes them curious. No question is too silly!

How did you do the research for this book?

I start by writing questions that I'd like the answers to. Some of these questions come from children, and others are from me. This helps me narrow down my research. If I tried to read EVERYTHING about poo, it would take too long and would muddle my brain! Once I have a list of questions, I search for answers. I look at science news and in scientific journals (special places where scientists write about their research for other scientists to read). Sometimes I speak to a scientist directly, to get their expert opinion.

What's the most amazing fact about poo that you discovered when researching this book?

I was amazed to discover that certain lobsters can eat jellyfish without being stung – they just poo out the deadly stingers!

Book chat

What did you think about the subject at the start? Did you change your mind about poo as as you read the book?

If you could change one thing about the book, what would it be?

If you had to give the book a new title, what would you choose?

Which fact about poo surprised you most? Why?

What did you like most about the book?

Would you recommend this book to a friend? Why/Why not?

Did this book remind you of any other books you have read?

89

Why do you think the book is called *Clues from Poos*?

What's the most interesting thing you've learned from reading this book?

If you could ask the author one question, what would you ask?

What animal's poo did you think was most interesting?

What fact about poo made you say "yuck"?

Do you think you could now be a poo detective and find clues from poos?

Do you think we might find more uses for poo in the future?

Book challenge:

Next time you're on a walk, try to find clues left behind by animals!

Collins
BIG CAT

Published by Collins
An imprint of HarperCollins*Publishers*
The News Building
1 London Bridge Street
London SE1 9GF
UK

Macken House
39/40 Mayor Street Upper
Dublin 1
D01 C9W8
Ireland

Author: Isabel Thomas
Publisher: Lizzie Catford
Product manager: Caroline Green
Series editor: Charlotte Raby
Commissioning editor: Suzannah Ditchburn
Development editor: Catherine Baker
Project manager: Emily Hooton
Content editor: Daniela Mora Chavarría
Copyeditor: Sally Byford
Proofreader: Gaynor Spry
Picture researcher: Sophie Hartley
Cover designer: 2Hoots Publishing Ltd
Typesetter: Banana Bear Books
Production controller: Katharine Willard

Download the teaching notes and word cards to accompany this book at: http://littlewandle.org.uk/signupfluency/

Get the latest Collins Big Cat news at collins.co.uk/collinsbigcat

MIX
Paper | Supporting responsible forestry
FSC
www.fsc.org
FSC™ C007454

This book is produced from independently certified FSC™ paper to ensure responsible forest management.

For more information visit: www.harpercollins.co.uk/green

Collins would like to thank the teachers and children at the following schools who took part in the trialling of Big Cat for Little Wandle Fluency: Burley And Woodhead Church of England Primary School; Chesterton Primary School; Lady Margaret Primary School; Little Sutton Primary School; Parsloes Primary School.

Printed and bound in the UK using 100% Renewable Electricity at Martins the Printers Ltd

Acknowledgements
The publishers gratefully acknowledge the permission granted to reproduce the copyright material in this book. Every effort has been made to trace copyright holders and to obtain their permission for the use of copyright material. The publishers will gladly receive any information enabling them to rectify any error or omission at the first opportunity.

Cover tl David Chapman/Alamy, tr Tony Wu/Nature Picture Library/Alamy, b Rudmer Zwerver/Shutterstock, pp3tl & 4tl & 54b Paul R. Sterry/Nature Photographers Ltd/Alamy, pp3tr & 4tcl & 54tr imageBROKER.com GmbH & Co. KG/Alamy, pp3cr& 5tl Adrian Davies/Nature Picture Library/Alamy, pp3bl & 5tcl & 54tl PAUL R. STERRY/Nature Photographers Ltd/Alamy, pp3br & 5bcr Dom Greves/Alamy, p5tcr AGAMI Photo Agency/Alamy, pp7b & 55tr Sibylle A. Möller/Alamy, p11t Blue Planet Archive/Alamy, p14 Buiten-Beeld/Alamy, p17t Ger Bosma/Alamy, p18 Dave Watts/Alamy, p19t shane partridge/Alamy, p19b Edwin Giesbers/Nature Picture Library/Alamy, p20 Michele Burgess/Alamy, p21 John Warburton-Lee Photography/Alamy, p22 Adisha Pramod/Alamy, p25 IMAGES@ARTIST-AT-LARGE/Alamy, pp32 & 55cr Alister Firth/Alamy, p34 Jason Ondreicka/Alamy, p35t B. Mete Uz/Alamy, p35b Miha Krofel/Alamy, p36b John Anderson/Alamy, p37t BIOSPHOTO/Alamy, p37b Indraneil Das/Alamy, p39 Ingo Arndt/Nature Picture Library/Alamy, p42 Wanuttapong suwannasilp/Alamy, p43 IndustryAndTravel/Alamy, p44 Tony Wu/Nature Picture Library/Alamy, p46b imageBROKER/Alamy, p48b AfriPics.com/Alamy, p49b © Jeremy Midgely Univ South Africa, p50 David Tipling Photo Library/Alamy, p53 Pictures From History/Universal Images Group/Getty Images, p57 Brent Stephenson/Nature Picture Library, p60 Stefan Rousseau/PA Images/Alamy, p63 ROGER HARRIS/SPL/Getty Images, p64 Alain Guilleux/Alamy, p66 Panther Media GmbH/Alamy, p67 Panther Media GmbH/Alamy, p6 8Holger Burmeister/Alamy, p72 a-plus imagebank/Alamy, p73 YAY Media AS/Alamy, p74 Jens Otte/Alamy, p76 Stephen Dwyer/Alamy, p77 Clearviewimages RF/Alamy, p80l Pictorial Press Ltd/Alamy, p80r Abbus Archive Images/Alamy, p81 Lordprice Collection/Alamy, p82 NASA, back cover (l) Seaphotoart/Alamy, back cover (r) Katja Forster/Shutterstock, all other photos Shutterstock.